Limitless:
Making Money with AI
By CJ Tate

Table of Contents

Chapter 1: Understanding Conversational AI

Conversational AI is a branch of artificial intelligence that focuses on creating systems capable of engaging in human-like conversations. It involves the use of natural language processing and machine learning techniques to understand and generate responses in a conversational manner. Over the years, Conversational AI has evolved from rule-based systems that followed predefined patterns to advanced language models that can generate coherent and contextually relevant responses.

Introducing ChatGPT

ChatGPT is an impressive example of Conversational AI developed by OpenAI. It is built upon the GPT (Generative Pre-trained Transformer) architecture, which enables it to understand and generate text based on the context provided. ChatGPT utilizes a large dataset of text from the internet to learn patterns and generate human-like responses. It can handle a wide range of conversational inputs and outputs, making it a versatile tool for various applications.

Getting Started with ChatGPT

To start using ChatGPT, you need to create an account and familiarize yourself with the user interface. The interface allows you to input prompts or questions to ChatGPT and view the generated responses. It's important to explore the different use cases of ChatGPT, such as interactive storytelling, digital consultancy, language learning, and many more, to understand the full potential of this powerful tool.

Leveraging ChatGPT for Interactive Storytelling and Digital Consultancy

Interactive storytelling is an exciting application of ChatGPT. By integrating ChatGPT into a narrative, you can create an immersive experience where readers actively engage with the story. Through a series of questions and choices, readers can influence the story's direction and enjoy a personalized narrative journey. For example, as a detective story unfolds, readers can interact with ChatGPT to gather clues and solve puzzles, enhancing their overall reading experience.

ChatGPT can also be a valuable tool in digital consultancy. It allows consultants to provide personalized recommendations and expert advice to clients in real-time. By integrating ChatGPT into consultancy services, businesses can enhance customer experience by offering interactive consultations. For instance, a digital consultant can utilize ChatGPT to provide tailored guidance on improving website SEO, social media strategies, or optimizing digital marketing campaigns.

Exploring New Frontiers with ChatGPT

The capabilities of ChatGPT extend beyond storytelling and consultancy. It can be utilized in various industries and applications to push boundaries and innovate. For instance, in language learning platforms, ChatGPT can facilitate interactive conversational lessons, providing learners with a realistic and engaging experience. By generating responses in the target language, giving feedback, and simulating conversations, ChatGPT enhances the language learning process.

In this introductory chapter, you've gained an understanding of ChatGPT and its potential applications in Conversational AI. From interactive storytelling to digital consultancy and beyond, ChatGPT opens up new possibilities for engaging and personalized experiences. As you proceed to the next chapters, you'll delve deeper into the practical implementation of A.I. and ChatGPT in various contexts, unlocking its full money-making potential.

Chapter 2: Potential for Lead Generation

Ladies and gentlemen, welcome to Chapter 2 of our journey towards unlocking the limitless potential of ChatGPT. In the previous chapter, we explored the foundation of ChatGPT and the incredible opportunities it offers. Today, we venture into the heart of business acumen, discovering how ChatGPT can revolutionize lead generation, taking your enterprise to heights previously unattainable.

The Power of ChatGPT: A Paradigm Shift in Lead Generation

Let's start by recognizing the magnitude of the transformation before us. The art of lead generation, once an arduous and resource-intensive process, has been catapulted into the digital age by ChatGPT. It's time to acknowledge the game-changing power of this AI marvel.

Traditionally, lead generation meant cold calls, email blasts, and generic marketing strategies. But the world has evolved, and so must our methods. ChatGPT steps into the arena as your tireless, 24/7 digital sales representative, engaging potential customers on your behalf, and capturing valuable information seamlessly.

Engaging Your Audience: ChatGPT as Your Virtual Sales Ally

Imagine a potential customer visiting your website, unsure of where to begin. Enter ChatGPT, armed with its conversational prowess and the ability to answer questions, provide recommendations, and address concerns. It doesn't just greet your visitors; it guides them through their journey, making them feel heard and valued.

ChatGPT, through its natural language understanding, makes interactions feel personal. It doesn't just respond; it engages. It doesn't merely collect data; it fosters relationships. Your potential leads will find themselves not just browsing but conversing, forming a bond with your brand in the process.

But it doesn't stop there. ChatGPT is not just a conversational wizard; it's also a data magician. It captures valuable information about your leads during these interactions. It learns their preferences, their pain points, and their desires. It's like having an intuitive salesperson who knows exactly what to say to win hearts and minds.

These insights are pure gold in your marketing arsenal. With ChatGPT's help, you can segment your leads effectively, tailor your messaging, and create personalized marketing campaigns that resonate on a profound level. You're not just shooting in the dark; you're targeting with pinpoint precision.

Nurturing Leads: The Personal Touch

Now, dear readers, here's where ChatGPT truly shines. It's not just about collecting leads; it's about nurturing them. It can send personalized follow-up messages, recommend relevant content, or even share exclusive offers, all while maintaining that personal touch. It's like having an empathetic, always-on customer care specialist.

ChatGPT doesn't forget. It remembers past interactions, ensuring that each follow-up feels like a continuation of a meaningful conversation rather than a cold sales pitch. It's about building trust, and trust is the currency of conversion.

Driving Conversions: From Leads to Loyal Customers

As we journey deeper into the world of ChatGPT, we realize that this AI marvel is not just a tool; it's a strategic partner. It's there to assist and enhance your lead generation efforts, to turn those leads into loyal customers.

Remember this: ChatGPT is not just a piece of software. It's your virtual emissary, your data virtuoso, and your personalization powerhouse. Embrace its potential, and the possibilities are boundless.

So, dear readers, fasten your seatbelts and get ready for the journey of a lifetime, as we delve deeper into the art of making money with A.I., enhanced by the genius of ChatGPT. Your business is on the cusp of transformation, and you're at the helm. The future is here, and it's bright.

Chapter 3: Crafting Compelling Marketing Content

In our previous chapters, we've seen the remarkable ways ChatGPT can revolutionize lead generation and engage your audience. Today, we delve into the heart of your marketing strategy, exploring how ChatGPT can be your creative partner in crafting captivating marketing content that not only informs but truly resonates with your target audience.

The Art of Marketing Content: A ChatGPT Revolution

Marketing content is more than just words on a page; it's the soul of your brand, the story that connects with your customers. In the past, creating this content required inspiration, creativity, and often, long hours of brainstorming. But now, with ChatGPT, you have an ingenious collaborator at your fingertips.

Traditionally, crafting marketing content was a painstaking process, like molding clay into a sculpture. But ChatGPT has redefined the art. It's as if you've discovered an unlimited palette of colors, a symphony of words, and a boundless well of inspiration. With ChatGPT, you can create content that not only informs but also evokes emotions, builds connections, and drives action.

Captivating Advertisements: ChatGPT's Creative Brilliance

Ad campaigns can make or break a brand. With ChatGPT's creative prowess, you can craft advertisements that stand out in a crowded marketplace. It understands the power of persuasion and knows how to use language to captivate your audience.

Imagine this: You run a small bakery, and you want to promote your new line of artisanal pastries. ChatGPT can help you craft a mouthwatering blog post that not only describes your pastries but transports the reader to a cozy café, savoring every bite. It's like having a creative genius as your personal content assistant.

Let's say you're marketing a luxury car. ChatGPT can generate ad copy that not only highlights the car's features but also tells a compelling story about the thrill of driving it. It creates headlines that grab attention, body text that keeps readers engaged, and calls to action that drive conversions. ChatGPT turns your marketing collateral into works of art.

Tailoring Messaging: Resonating with Your Audience

One size doesn't fit all in marketing. Different audiences require different approaches. ChatGPT excels at tailoring messaging to resonate with specific demographics or personas.

Imagine you have an online fitness app, and you want to target two distinct audiences: young adults looking to get fit and older individuals seeking low-impact exercises. ChatGPT can help you craft marketing emails that speak directly to each group, using the right language, tone, and offers. It's like having a marketing strategist who knows your customers inside out.

Brand Recognition: Building a Lasting Impression

Consistency is key in branding. ChatGPT can assist you in maintaining a consistent brand voice across all channels, ensuring that your audience instantly recognizes your brand's identity.

Let's take a coffee shop chain, for instance. ChatGPT can analyze your existing content, understand your brand's personality, and suggest ways to make your social media posts, email newsletters, and website copy align seamlessly. It becomes your brand's guardian, ensuring every piece of content leaves a lasting impression.

Examples of ChatGPT in Action

Here are real-world examples of businesses leveraging ChatGPT:

- Netflix: ChatGPT powers recommendation algorithms, suggesting shows and movies that match users' preferences.
- Shopify: Shopify's ChatGPT-driven chatbot helps e-commerce store owners with customer inquiries, enhancing user experience.
- Grammarly: Grammarly's AI writing assistant uses ChatGPT technology to provide real-time grammar and style suggestions to users.

In conclusion, ChatGPT isn't just a tool; it's your creative companion in the world of marketing. As we delve deeper into this realm in the upcoming chapters, remember that ChatGPT amplifies your ideas and brings your brand to life. The future of content marketing is here, and ChatGPT is your ticket to crafting compelling content that resonates and drives results. Stay tuned for more insights and strategies!

Chapter 4: Revolutionizing Digital Publications

In the previous chapters, we explored the transformative power of ChatGPT in lead generation and marketing content creation. Today, we embark on a new adventure, one that takes us into the world of digital publications and how ChatGPT is revolutionizing this landscape.

The Evolution of Digital Publications

Digital publications have come a long way since their inception. Gone are the days of static PDFs and plain web articles. In this digital age, users expect interactive and engaging experiences. The question is, how can you breathe new life into traditional publications and captivate your audience in this dynamic era?

ChatGPT emerges as the answer to this question. Imagine transforming a static, text-heavy article into an immersive, interactive journey. Let's take a look at a real-world example:

Example 1: The Interactive Travel Magazine

Imagine you're the editor of a travel magazine, and you want to feature a destination in an upcoming issue. With ChatGPT, you can create an interactive article that allows readers to explore the destination in a whole new way.

Dynamic Content Generation

ChatGPT can generate dynamic content for your article, providing historical insights, travel tips, and even personalized recommendations based on the reader's interests. It scours the web for the latest information about the destination, ensuring that your content is up-to-date and relevant. This dynamic approach turns your article into a valuable resource that readers can return to again and again.

Multimedia Integration

To make your travel article truly engaging, ChatGPT can seamlessly integrate multimedia elements. It can embed interactive maps that allow readers to explore the destination's landmarks and attractions. High-quality images and videos can transport readers to the destination, immersing them in the experience. With ChatGPT's assistance, your travel article becomes more than words on a page — it becomes a virtual journey.

Real-time Conversations

But what truly sets ChatGPT apart is its ability to engage readers in real-time conversations. Through natural language processing, ChatGPT can answer readers' questions and provide personalized travel recommendations. Readers no longer passively consume information; they actively participate in a conversation with your publication. This level of interactivity creates a deeper connection between your brand and the audience.

By harnessing the power of ChatGPT, you've transformed a traditional article into an interactive and immersive experience that keeps readers coming back for more. Your publication becomes a trusted companion for travelers, providing not just information but a personalized guide to their adventures.

Dynamic Content Generation

One of the most exciting aspects of ChatGPT is its ability to generate dynamic content on the fly. Whether you're a news organization, a content aggregator, or a blogger, ChatGPT can be your go-to tool for generating fresh and relevant articles.

Example 2: The Newsroom of the Future

Imagine you're the editor-in-chief of a news website. You want to provide your readers with the latest updates on a breaking news story. ChatGPT can assist in several ways:

Real-time Updates

It can monitor news feeds and social media for real-time updates, ensuring your article is always up-to-date. This capability is invaluable in the fast-paced world of news where every second counts. With ChatGPT as your digital newsroom assistant, you can be confident that your readers receive the most current information.

Dynamic Summaries

ChatGPT can generate concise and informative news summaries, allowing you to cover multiple angles of a story quickly. It extracts key information from various sources, condenses it into a coherent summary, and presents it in an easily digestible format. This not only saves your editorial team time but also provides readers with clear and comprehensive news coverage.

Personalized Briefings

But ChatGPT's capabilities go beyond traditional news reporting. It can even draft personalized news briefings for individual readers, tailoring content to their interests and preferences. Let's say you have a reader who's particularly interested in technology and sports. ChatGPT can curate a briefing that highlights the latest tech developments and sports scores, delivering a tailored news experience.

With ChatGPT as your digital newsroom assistant, you're not just reporting the news; you're delivering a dynamic and personalized news experience. Readers get the information they need, when they need it, in a format that suits their preferences. It's a win-win situation that keeps readers engaged and informed.

AI-Driven Recommendations

In the digital publishing world, recommendations play a vital role in keeping users engaged. ChatGPT can take your recommendation system to the next level by understanding user preferences and offering highly relevant suggestions.

Example 3: The Personalized Content Platform

Imagine you run a content platform that covers a wide range of topics, from technology to lifestyle. ChatGPT can analyze user behavior and preferences to provide personalized recommendations:

Understanding User Interests

It can understand what topics a user is interested in based on their reading history and interactions. Let's say a user frequently reads articles about fitness and healthy eating. ChatGPT can identify these preferences and use them as a foundation for content recommendations.

Generating Personalized Suggestions

ChatGPT can then generate personalized content suggestions, tailoring the platform's homepage to each user's unique tastes. It presents articles, videos, and other content that align with the user's interests. This level of personalization enhances the user experience, making your platform more valuable to each visitor.

Dynamic Content Previews

But ChatGPT doesn't stop at recommendations. It can provide dynamic content previews, giving users a glimpse of what they can expect from articles before they click. For instance, if a user is interested in a particular tech article, ChatGPT can generate a brief summary or highlight key points, helping the user decide if it's worth exploring further.

With ChatGPT's AI-driven recommendations, your content platform becomes a personalized oasis of information, ensuring users stay engaged and find value in every visit. Users no longer have to sift through a sea of content to find what they're interested in — it's delivered to them on a silver platter.

The Future of Digital Publications

As we journey deeper into the world of digital publications enhanced by ChatGPT, it becomes clear that the future is bright. The days of static, one-size-fits-all content are behind us. With ChatGPT, we're ushering in an era of dynamic, interactive, and personalized digital experiences.

Imagine the possibilities: textbooks that adapt to a student's learning style, scientific journals that explain complex concepts in plain language, or cooking magazines that provide real-time ingredient substitutions. ChatGPT is the key to unlocking these possibilities.

In education, ChatGPT can assist educators in creating personalized learning materials. It can generate interactive quizzes and provide real-time explanations of complex topics, catering to each student's individual needs.

In academia, ChatGPT can help researchers sift through vast amounts of data and literature to identify relevant sources, accelerating the research process and driving scientific discoveries.

In e-commerce, ChatGPT can assist customers in finding the perfect products based on their preferences and needs. It can generate product descriptions, answer questions, and provide personalized recommendations, leading to higher customer satisfaction and increased sales.

In healthcare, ChatGPT can aid healthcare professionals in diagnosing medical conditions, providing treatment recommendations, and offering patient education materials. It can be a valuable tool in telemedicine, bridging the gap between patients and healthcare providers.

In customer support, ChatGPT can handle routine inquiries, freeing up human agents to focus on more complex issues. It can provide instant answers to frequently asked questions and guide customers through troubleshooting processes.

In content creation, ChatGPT can assist writers, journalists, and content creators by generating ideas, providing research assistance, and even suggesting improvements to drafts. It's a collaborator that enhances creativity and productivity.

A Revolution in the Making

In this chapter, we've scratched the surface of how ChatGPT is revolutionizing digital publications. We've seen how it can transform static content into dynamic experiences, generate fresh articles, and provide AI-driven recommendations.

As you continue to explore the potential of ChatGPT in the realm of digital publications, keep in mind that the journey is just beginning. The future holds even more exciting innovations and applications for this incredible technology. The possibilities are endless, and with ChatGPT by your side, you're on the cusp of a publishing revolution.

The key takeaway from this chapter is that ChatGPT is not just a tool; it's a transformative force that can reshape the way we create and consume digital content. It empowers publishers, educators, researchers, and businesses to deliver more engaging, personalized, and valuable experiences to their audiences.

As we continue our journey with ChatGPT, stay tuned for more insights, case studies, and strategies that will help you unlock the full potential of this remarkable AI technology in the realm of digital publications. The future is bright, and ChatGPT is leading the way.

Chapter 5: Mastering the Art of Blogging

Ladies and gentlemen, welcome to Chapter 4 of our enthralling journey into the realm of ChatGPT. We've embarked on a captivating odyssey, uncovering the transformative potential of ChatGPT in lead generation, marketing content, digital publications, and more. In this chapter, we dive deep into the world of blogging, exploring how ChatGPT can be your guiding star in mastering the art of crafting captivating blog posts.

The Power of Words

Blogging is an art, a dynamic blend of creativity, passion, and storytelling prowess. The written word possesses an extraordinary power—it can educate, inspire, entertain, and, most importantly, connect with readers on a profound level. It's the digital age's equivalent of the age-old campfire tales, drawing readers into your world, and inviting them to share in your experiences. But, let's be honest, crafting engaging and memorable blog posts is no small feat.

In the era of short attention spans and a glut of content, your blog must not merely survive; it must thrive. It must offer true value, captivate your readers, and leave them eagerly awaiting your next post. This is where ChatGPT emerges as your invaluable ally.

Unleashing ChatGPT's Writing Prowess

Picture having a tireless writing assistant, immune to the ravages of writer's block, and armed with an encyclopedic knowledge of nearly every subject. ChatGPT is that steadfast ally, ready to help you craft blog posts that are not merely informative but captivating and engaging to boot.

Example 1: The Travel Blog

Let's embark on a journey into the world of travel blogging. Imagine you're a passionate traveler, eager to share your adventures and discoveries with the world. However, translating the breathtaking beauty and wonder of your destinations into words often proves challenging.

This is where ChatGPT steps in as your indispensable travel companion. Here's how it can assist:

Engaging Introductions

One of the critical elements of a successful travel blog post is capturing your reader's attention right from the beginning. ChatGPT excels at generating captivating introductions that hook readers instantly. Whether you're describing the enchantment of an exotic location or the thrill of a daring adventure, ChatGPT sets the stage for an immersive reading experience.

Informative Content

ChatGPT's vast repository of knowledge transforms it into a highly efficient research assistant. It can provide historical context, fascinating facts, and practical travel tips, enriching your blog posts. With ChatGPT's assistance, your travel blog doesn't merely narrate your experiences; it provides readers with a comprehensive and authentic guide to the destinations.

Conversational Tone

Maintaining an engaging and relatable tone in your blog posts can be a challenge. ChatGPT's natural language capabilities help you strike just the right chord. It ensures that readers feel as if they're having a friendly chat with you, transforming dry facts into captivating stories.

It's akin to having a trusted friend recount their adventures.

With ChatGPT's writing prowess at your disposal, your travel blog transcends being a mere collection of stories; it becomes an inviting journey, a portal through which readers experience the thrill of exploration, even from the comfort of their own homes.

Developing a Content Strategy

Creating captivating blog posts is only one facet of successful blogging. To thrive in the blogosphere, you need a well-thought-out content strategy that aligns with your target audience's interests and desires. ChatGPT can serve as your strategic partner in this endeavor.

Example 2: The Tech Blog

Imagine running a tech blog catering to tech enthusiasts hungry for the latest industry developments. To keep your readers engaged and returning for more, your content strategy must encompass a mix of news updates, in-depth analyses, and practical tech tips.

Generating Fresh Ideas

ChatGPT is not merely a writing tool; it's a creative brainstorming companion. It can generate a curated list of fresh blog post ideas based on trending topics, feedback from your audience, and insights from within the tech industry. It ensures that your content remains relevant, engaging, and always aligned with your readers' interests.

Audience Understanding

Understanding your audience is the foundation of creating content that resonates. ChatGPT can sift through reader comments, social media interactions, and feedback to glean insights into what your audience craves. Armed with these insights, you can tailor your content to their specific interests and concerns, ensuring your blog remains a go-to resource.

Editorial Calendar

A well-structured editorial calendar is indispensable for maintaining a consistent and engaging blog. ChatGPT can assist in creating a content calendar that outlines topics, publication dates, and deadlines. This helps you keep your posting schedule on track, ensuring a regular stream of high-quality content that keeps your audience informed and engaged.

With ChatGPT as your content strategy partner, your tech blog transcends being merely informative; it becomes a trusted source of information and insights. You're not just reporting on tech news; you're providing valuable perspectives and solutions to your readers, establishing your blog as a vital resource in the tech community.

Enhancing SEO with ChatGPT

Search Engine Optimization (SEO) is the backbone of a successful blog. It's the art of making your blog posts discoverable by search engines like Google, ensuring that they rank high in search results. ChatGPT can play a significant role in enhancing your blog's SEO performance.

Example 3: The Lifestyle Blog

Consider a lifestyle blog that covers a wide array of topics, from fashion to wellness. To attract organic traffic and achieve high rankings on search engine results pages (SERPs), you need a robust SEO strategy.

Keyword Research

Keyword research is the bedrock of effective SEO. ChatGPT can assist in this critical task by identifying relevant keywords and phrases that align with the content of your blog posts. This ensures that your blog posts are optimized for search, making it easier for readers to discover your content when searching online.

SEO-Friendly Content

Crafting SEO-friendly content is an art in itself. It involves seamlessly integrating keywords, optimizing headings, and adhering to other SEO best practices. ChatGPT can generate blog posts that incorporate keywords naturally and follow SEO guidelines, making certain that your content not only appeals to readers but also ranks favorably on search engines.

Meta Descriptions

Meta descriptions are often the first thing potential readers see when your blog post appears in search results. ChatGPT can assist in crafting compelling meta descriptions that entice users to click on your blog posts. It's akin to having a virtual copywriter who specializes in metadata, making certain that your blog posts receive the attention they deserve.

By harnessing ChatGPT's capabilities, your lifestyle blog doesn't merely thrive; it becomes a magnet for organic traffic. You're not just producing outstanding content; you're ensuring that it reaches the right audience through search engines. This elevates your blog's visibility and impact, positioning it as a trusted source of lifestyle insights.

The Artistry of Blogging

In this chapter, we've embarked on an illuminating journey into how ChatGPT can be your guiding star in mastering the art of blogging. We've witnessed how it can unleash its writing prowess to create captivating blog posts, assist in the development of a content strategy, and enhance SEO efforts.

However, it's essential to remember that blogging is not solely about algorithms and keywords; it's about connecting with your audience, sharing your passions, and leaving a lasting impact. ChatGPT is a tool — an incredibly potent one — but the true artistry of blogging lies within you, your unique voice, your experiences, and your perspective.

As you continue your blogging expedition with ChatGPT as your trusted companion, keep in mind that it's not a replacement for your creativity; it's an amplifier. It takes your ideas, your vision, and your storytelling to new heights. With ChatGPT by your side, your blog becomes a canvas upon which you paint vivid stories, share valuable insights, and engage readers in meaningful conversations.

The future of blogging is here, and it's powered by ChatGPT. As we continue our exploration of this remarkable AI technology, stay tuned for further insights, case studies, and strategies that will assist you in elevating your blogging to unparalleled heights. The artistry of blogging awaits, and ChatGPT stands as your trusted guide through this captivating journey.

Chapter 6: Maximizing Revenue

Up to this point, we've explored the incredible potential of ChatGPT in lead generation, marketing content, and digital publications. Now, it's time to venture into the realm of revenue generation. In this chapter, we'll delve deep into the art of maximizing revenue through effective monetization strategies, turning your ChatGPT-powered ventures into profitable enterprises that thrive.

The Quest for Revenue

While innovation and creativity drive many ventures, financial sustainability remains a crucial pillar of success. In the context of ChatGPT-powered projects like lead generation, marketing content, and digital publications, finding the right monetization strategies is paramount for long-term viability.

The challenge goes beyond generating revenue; it lies in doing so while enhancing the user experience and delivering genuine value. This chapter explores a range of monetization models and strategies that will help you strike that delicate balance.

Monetization Models for ChatGPT-Powered Ventures

Before we dive into the specifics, let's first explore the fundamental monetization models that can be applied to ChatGPT-powered ventures.

Lead Generation

In the realm of lead generation, your primary goal is to capture and qualify leads for your business or clients. While this service can be valuable in itself, there are several monetization approaches to consider:

- Pay-Per-Lead (PPL)
    - Under this model, you charge businesses or clients for each qualified lead generated through ChatGPT interactions.
    - The pricing can vary based on lead quality and industry competitiveness. For instance, in the real estate sector, high-quality leads may command a higher PPL rate.
- Subscription-Based Services
    - In addition to PPL, you can offer subscription-based lead generation services.

- o Clients pay a regular fee to access a consistent stream of leads.
- o This model provides steady revenue while ensuring a stable lead flow for clients.

Marketing Content

Marketing content generated by ChatGPT can be a valuable asset for businesses looking to enhance their online presence and engage with their audience. Monetization in this domain can take various forms:

- Content Licensing
    - o You can license the marketing content generated by ChatGPT to businesses seeking ready-made content for their websites, blogs, or social media.
    - o The pricing structure can be based on usage, with businesses paying for the number of articles, blog posts, or social media updates they deploy.
- Sponsored Content
    - o Another avenue is to collaborate with businesses on sponsored content.

- o This involves creating content specifically tailored to promote a product or service.
- o The business compensates you for both content creation and exposure to your audience.

Digital Publications

Digital publications enhanced by ChatGPT offer unique opportunities for monetization. These can include interactive magazines, news platforms, or educational resources. Let's explore the various ways to monetize digital publications:

- Advertising
    - o Displaying advertisements within your digital publication is a classic monetization method.
    - o You can partner with ad networks or directly with advertisers to place ads.
    - o Advertisers pay based on impressions (CPM), clicks (CPC), or actions (CPA).
- Partnerships
    - o Collaborating with businesses, organizations, or influencers can be mutually beneficial.

- o Partnerships can involve co-creating content, cross-promotions, or joint events.
- o These arrangements often come with financial benefits or revenue-sharing agreements.
- Sponsored Content
  - o Similar to marketing content, you can feature sponsored content within your digital publication.
  - o Businesses or brands pay for the creation and placement of content that aligns with their goals and interests your audience.
- Subscription-Based Models
  - o Subscriptions are a potent monetization approach, providing exclusive access and additional value to subscribers.
  - o Whether you're operating in the realm of lead generation, marketing content, or digital publications, subscription-based models can be tailored to your specific offering.
- Premium Access
  - o Offer premium access to enhanced features, personalized

content, or advanced capabilities of your ChatGPT-powered service.

- o Subscribers pay a regular fee to enjoy these benefits.
- Content Libraries
  - o For digital publications, consider creating extensive content libraries.
  - o Subscribers gain access to a vast archive of valuable articles, reports, or resources, enriching their experience.

Now that we've explored these monetization models, let's delve into strategies that can help you maximize revenue in your ChatGPT-powered ventures.

Leveraging Advertising for Revenue

Advertising is a tried-and-true monetization strategy that can be harnessed across various ChatGPT-powered ventures. Whether you're operating a lead generation platform, generating marketing content, or running a digital publication, advertising revenue can significantly contribute to your financial success.

Strategy 1: Targeted Advertising

Incorporate data-driven insights from ChatGPT to offer highly targeted advertising opportunities. Leverage ChatGPT's understanding of user behavior and preferences to provide advertisers with precise audience targeting options. This not only increases the effectiveness of advertisements but also enhances their value, allowing you to command higher ad rates.

Strategy 2: Native Advertising

Native advertising seamlessly integrates sponsored content within the user experience, making it less intrusive and more engaging. Incorporate ChatGPT-generated native ads that blend harmoniously with your platform's content, ensuring a smoother user experience while delivering value to advertisers.

Strategy 3: Programmatic Advertising

Implement programmatic advertising systems that use artificial intelligence to automate the buying of ads and optimize their placement. ChatGPT can analyze user data in real-time, helping you maximize ad revenues by displaying the most relevant ads to each user.

Partnering for Profit

Collaborations and partnerships can be potent tools in your monetization arsenal. Whether you're focusing on lead generation, marketing content, or digital publications, forging the right partnerships can unlock new revenue streams.

Strategy 4: Content Syndication

Partner with other content creators, platforms, or media outlets to syndicate your ChatGPT-generated content. This expands your reach and exposes your content to new audiences, potentially resulting in revenue-sharing arrangements.

Strategy 5: Affiliate Marketing

Incorporate affiliate marketing into your monetization strategy. Promote relevant products or services within your content or platform and earn commissions on sales generated through your referral links. ChatGPT can assist in identifying suitable affiliate opportunities based on user behavior and preferences.

Strategy 6: Co-Branded Content

Explore co-branded content opportunities with businesses or influencers in your niche. Create content that serves both parties' interests and is sponsored by the partner. These collaborations can come with financial benefits and increased exposure.

Sponsored Content: A Lucrative Avenue

Sponsored content presents an enticing revenue stream across a range of ChatGPT-powered ventures. By strategically incorporating sponsored content, you can monetize your platform while maintaining the quality and integrity of your offerings.

Strategy 7: Maintaining Relevance

Ensure that sponsored content aligns seamlessly with your platform's theme and interests. ChatGPT can play a pivotal role in generating sponsored content that resonates with your audience, maintaining the overall quality and authenticity of your platform.

Strategy 8: Transparency

Maintain transparency with your audience regarding sponsored content. Clearly label sponsored posts or content to maintain trust with your readers or users. An honest approach ensures the continued credibility of your platform.

Strategy 9: Diversification

Diversify your sponsored content offerings. Explore different formats, such as articles, videos, webinars, or podcasts, to cater to varying advertiser needs and preferences. ChatGPT can assist in creating diverse sponsored content assets.

Subscription-Based Models: Providing Exclusive Value

Subscription-based models are a compelling way to monetize your ChatGPT-powered venture. By offering exclusive access and additional value to subscribers, you can create a steady stream of revenue while enhancing the user experience.

Strategy 10: Freemium Models

Implement freemium models that offer both free and premium tiers. Free users can access basic features, while premium subscribers enjoy advanced capabilities, personalized content, and an ad-free experience. ChatGPT can assist in tailoring content to premium subscribers, enhancing their experience.

Strategy 11: Content Bundles

Create content bundles that provide subscribers with access to a curated selection of premium content or features. Offer these bundles at a compelling price point to incentivize subscription sign-ups.

Strategy 12: Early Access

Provide early access to new features, content, or updates to your subscribers. This not only rewards their loyalty but also encourages others to subscribe to gain access to exclusive benefits.

Case Studies in Monetization Success

To illustrate the effectiveness of these monetization strategies in ChatGPT-powered ventures, let's delve into a few case studies:

Case Study 1: The Lead Generation Platform

A lead generation platform specializing in connecting businesses with potential customers implemented a subscription-based model. They offered businesses a choice between pay-per-lead and a monthly subscription. The subscription option provided businesses with a predictable lead flow and access to premium leads. The result? Increased revenue stability and higher lifetime customer value.

Case Study 2: The Marketing Content Generator

A marketing content generator leveraged targeted advertising within its user dashboard. Using ChatGPT's user insights, they offered advertisers highly specific targeting options, resulting in a 25% increase in ad rates. Additionally, they incorporated native advertising seamlessly into their content, improving the user experience and attracting more advertisers.

Case Study 3: The Digital Publication

A digital publication diversified its revenue streams by partnering with industry influencers. They co-created content that appealed to both their audience and the influencer's followers. This resulted in increased exposure and higher advertising rates. The publication also introduced a premium subscription tier, offering exclusive access to in-depth reports and live webinars. The subscription base grew steadily, providing a reliable source of income.

Monetization Mastery

In this chapter, we've embarked on a journey to master the art of monetization in ChatGPT-powered ventures. We explored various monetization models, including lead generation, marketing content, and digital publications, and delved into strategies such as advertising, partnerships, and sponsored content.

As you chart your course in the world of ChatGPT-powered ventures, remember that successful monetization is not about quick gains but about building sustainable revenue streams that align with your users' needs and expectations. By implementing the right strategies, forging strategic partnerships, and offering exclusive value through subscriptions, you can unlock the full potential of your ChatGPT-powered venture and ensure its long-term financial success.

Chapter 7: Cultivating a Strong Online Presence and Audience Engagement

We've traversed a myriad of domains, from lead generation to monetization strategies, and now, we embark on an exciting quest to master the art of cultivating a robust online presence and igniting audience engagement — an art that will breathe life into your ChatGPT-powered endeavors.

The Essence of Online Presence

In this digital age, your online presence is not just a mere reflection of your brand; it's a living, breathing entity that can enchant, engage, and build enduring relationships with your audience. Imagine it as your digital personality, the gateway through which you connect with the world.

In this chapter, we'll unveil the secrets to crafting a compelling online presence and dive into strategies that will set your venture apart in the crowded digital arena.

Effective Social Media Strategies

Social media platforms are the bustling marketplaces of the digital realm — a place where potential customers, avid readers, and passionate followers congregate. To stand out in this bustling landscape, you need more than a presence; you need a well-crafted strategy.

Strategy 1: Know Your Platforms

Not all social media platforms are created equal. Each has its unique audience, culture, and strengths. To maximize your online presence, start by understanding where your target audience hangs out. Are they scrolling through Instagram's visual delights, sharing thoughts on Twitter, making professional connections on LinkedIn, or dancing through the world of TikTok? Tailor your approach to each platform, ensuring your content resonates with its users.

Strategy 2: The Rhythm of Consistency

Consistency is the secret ingredient to making a mark in the digital universe. Whether you're posting blog updates, insightful market analyses, or interactive ChatGPT experiences, maintain a regular posting schedule. This not only keeps your audience engaged but also ensures you remain top-of-mind in an era of constant distractions.

Strategy 3: Engage Authentically

Remember, social media is not a one-way megaphone; it's a two-way conversation. Engage with your audience authentically. Respond to comments, answer questions, and actively participate in discussions related to your niche. When your audience sees that you're genuinely interested in their thoughts and opinions, they'll be more likely to engage with your content.

Strategy 4: Visual Storytelling

In a world overflowing with information, visual content reigns supreme. Use compelling visuals to tell your story. Whether it's captivating infographics, engaging videos, or eye-catching graphics, visuals have the power to convey your message swiftly and memorably.

Strategy 5: ChatGPT as a Conversation Catalyst

Leverage ChatGPT's conversational abilities to engage your audience. Create interactive experiences that encourage users to participate. For instance, run polls or surveys related to your niche and let ChatGPT facilitate the conversation. This not only boosts engagement but also provides valuable insights into your audience's preferences and needs.

Fostering Meaningful Connections

Beyond the glitz and glamour of social media, fostering meaningful connections with your audience is the cornerstone of a strong online presence. It's not just about having followers; it's about having true supporters who resonate with your vision and what you offer.

Strategy 6: Personalized Experiences

ChatGPT's prowess in personalization can be a game-changer. Use it to provide tailored recommendations, content, or solutions to your audience. When users feel that your ChatGPT-powered service understands and caters to their specific needs, they're more likely to return and engage consistently.

Strategy 7: Value-Driven Content

Value should be at the forefront of your content strategy. Whether you're generating leads, producing marketing content, or running a digital publication, your content should educate, entertain, or solve problems for your audience. When your audience consistently finds value in what you offer, they become loyal followers.

Strategy 8: Interactive Experiences

ChatGPT's interactivity can set you apart in the digital wilderness. Create quizzes, challenges, or games that involve ChatGPT. These interactive experiences not only engage users but also inject an element of fun and novelty into your online presence.

Strategy 9: Virtual Events

In our increasingly virtual world, hosting online events can be a powerful engagement tool. Whether it's webinars, live Q&A sessions, or virtual conferences, these events allow you to connect with your audience in real-time, fostering a sense of community and belonging.

Leveraging Community Feedback

Your audience is more than just spectators; they are your compass, your guiding star. Their feedback is the North Star that directs your journey. Embrace community feedback as a treasure trove of insights to refine and enhance your ChatGPT-powered offerings.

Strategy 10: Listen Actively

Listen with intent to what your audience is saying. Monitor comments, messages, and discussions related to your brand or service.

ChatGPT can assist in parsing this data, helping you uncover valuable insights and identify areas for improvement.

Strategy 11: Feedback Loops

Implement feedback loops that encourage users to share their thoughts and suggestions. Whether it's through surveys, feedback forms, or direct messages, make it effortless for your audience to provide input. ChatGPT can help automate these processes, making it convenient for users to share their opinions.

Strategy 12: Co-Creation

Consider co-creation initiatives where you collaborate with your audience to develop new features, content, or improvements to your ChatGPT-powered service. By involving your users in the creative process, you not only gather valuable input but also build a sense of ownership and loyalty within your community.

Case Studies in Audience Engagement

To illustrate the power of these strategies in cultivating a strong online presence and audience engagement, let's journey through a few captivating case studies:

Case Study 1: The Content Platform

A content platform that harnessed ChatGPT to generate educational content implemented an interactive quiz feature. Users could delve into quizzes spanning various topics, with ChatGPT providing personalized feedback and recommendations based on their quiz results. The platform encouraged users to share their quiz results on social media, creating a viral loop. Engagement skyrocketed, with users spending more time on the platform and eagerly sharing it with their networks.

Case Study 2: The Digital Magazine

A digital magazine, elevated by ChatGPT's prowess, adopted an innovative approach to audience engagement. They hosted monthly virtual events, featuring expert panels and live Q&A sessions. These events not only attracted a dedicated audience but also offered a unique opportunity for readers to interact with the authors and experts featured in the magazine. This interactive approach transformed passive readers into active participants, driving both engagement and subscriptions.

Case Study 3: The ChatGPT-Powered Community

A ChatGPT-powered community platform embraced the power of feedback loops. They implemented a chatbot-driven system that periodically checked in with users, asking for feedback and suggestions. Additionally, they hosted a monthly "Community Ideas Contest," where users could submit their ideas for platform improvements. The best ideas were implemented, and the users who submitted them received recognition and rewards. This approach not only improved the platform but also fostered a sense of ownership and belonging among community members.

The Heartbeat of Online Presence

In this chapter, we've unveiled the heart of cultivating a robust online presence and sparking audience engagement. Your online presence is not just a digital footprint; it's the soul of your venture, breathing life into your brand. By implementing effective social media strategies, fostering meaningful connections, and leveraging community feedback, you can create an online presence that captivates and endears your audience.

As we continue our voyage, the spotlight turns to the paramount importance of ethics in AI and ChatGPT-powered businesses. Join us in the next chapter for a thought-provoking exploration of responsible AI usage and the guiding principles that will lead you toward ethical excellence in this dynamic landscape. The journey continues, and the best is yet to come!

Chapter 8: Enhancing Customer Support

Welcome, dear readers, to the eighth chapter of our transformative journey through the realm of ChatGPT. We've navigated the intricacies of lead generation, explored the art of blogging, and even ventured into monetization strategies. Now, our path leads us to an essential aspect of any successful business: customer support. In this chapter, we will unveil the remarkable ways in which ChatGPT can enhance customer support, providing efficient and personalized experiences that leave customers delighted.

The Essence of Exceptional Customer Support

Customer support is the beating heart of any business. It's the frontline where customers interact with your brand, voice their concerns, and seek assistance. In today's digital age, the quality of customer support isn't just a matter of satisfaction; it's a strategic advantage that can set your business apart from the competition.

Enter ChatGPT, a versatile tool that can revolutionize how you provide customer support. Its capabilities allow you to offer efficient, personalized, and round-the-clock assistance. In this chapter, we'll explore the strategies and tactics to harness the full potential of ChatGPT in elevating your customer support game.

Utilizing ChatGPT for Personalized Experiences

Strategy 1: Personalized Responses

In the era of personalization, one-size-fits-all responses are a thing of the past. With ChatGPT, you can craft responses that are tailored to the specific needs and inquiries of each customer. This level of personalization makes customers feel valued and understood.

For instance, imagine a customer contacting an e-commerce website with a query about a specific product. ChatGPT, armed with information about the customer's browsing history and preferences, can provide product recommendations that are highly relevant to their interests. This not only answers the customer's query but also potentially leads to a sale.

Strategy 2: Contextual Conversations

Have you ever been frustrated by having to repeat the same information to customer support multiple times? ChatGPT can retain context throughout a conversation, allowing it to provide relevant responses based on previous interactions. This not only saves time but also creates a seamless and personalized experience for the customer.

For instance, a customer contacts a tech support chatbot with an issue regarding their smartphone. After a brief exchange, the customer has to leave the conversation and returns later. ChatGPT remembers the previous conversation and continues assisting the customer with the same issue, eliminating the need to re-explain the problem.

Strategy 3: Multilingual Support

In our globalized world, providing support in multiple languages is no longer a luxury but a necessity. ChatGPT's language capabilities can break down language barriers, ensuring that customers from diverse linguistic backgrounds receive the assistance they need.

Consider a scenario where a multinational company uses ChatGPT-powered chatbots to provide support on its website. These chatbots can seamlessly switch between languages based on the user's preference, making the support experience smoother and more accessible for a global audience.

Strategy 4: Automating Routine Queries

Frequently asked questions can be a drain on human resources. ChatGPT-powered chatbots can efficiently handle routine queries, freeing up your human support team to focus on more complex issues. This not only boosts efficiency but also ensures that customers receive quick responses, even during peak support hours.

Imagine an airline using ChatGPT-powered chatbots to handle common customer inquiries such as baggage policies, flight schedules, and booking changes. This allows the human support team to dedicate their expertise to more intricate issues like flight disruptions or complex bookings, improving overall customer satisfaction.

Implementing Chatbots with ChatGPT

Now, let's delve deeper into the practical aspects of creating chatbots with ChatGPT to enhance your customer support capabilities:

- Step 1: Define the Purpose
  - Before diving into chatbot creation, clearly define the

purpose and scope of your
chatbot.
- o What specific tasks or inquiries
will it handle?
- o Will it provide support on your
website, app, or social media
platforms?
- o Understanding its role is crucial
for effective implementation.
- Step 2: Data Gathering
- o Collect the data and information
necessary for your chatbot to
function effectively.
- o This includes frequently asked
questions, product details,
troubleshooting guides, and any
other relevant content.
- o Ensure that the data is well-
organized and accessible for
integration.
- Step 3: Choose the Right Platform
- o Select a chatbot development
platform that aligns with your
business's needs and technical
capabilities.
- o Several platforms, such as
Dialogflow, Microsoft Bot
Framework, and IBM Watson
Assistant, offer user-friendly

interfaces for chatbot creation
and integration.

- Step 4: Design the Conversation Flow
  - o Map out the conversation flow
    and dialogues that your chatbot
    will use to interact with
    customers.
  - o Consider different user scenarios
    and design responses that
    provide clear and helpful
    information.
  - o Ensure that the chatbot can
    handle unexpected user inputs
    gracefully.
- Step 5: Integration with ChatGPT
  - o Integrate ChatGPT's language
    model into your chatbot
    platform.
  - o Most modern chatbot
    development platforms offer
    APIs (Application Programming
    Interfaces) that allow you to
    connect ChatGPT for natural
    language processing and
    responses.
- Step 6: Testing and Iteration
  - o Thoroughly test your chatbot to
    identify and iron out any issues.

- o Encourage team members to interact with the chatbot as if they were customers to ensure it provides a seamless experience.
- o Collect feedback and iterate on the chatbot's design and responses to improve its performance.
- Step 7: Deployment and Monitoring
  - o Once your chatbot is ready, deploy it on your chosen customer support channels.
  - o Monitor its interactions and collect data on user satisfaction, response times, and common inquiries.
  - o Use this data to further refine your chatbot's performance over time.

Implementing Chatbots and Virtual Assistants

Strategy 5: 24/7 Availability

Customers don't keep regular business hours, and their inquiries can come at any time. Chatbots and virtual assistants powered by ChatGPT can provide round-the-clock support, ensuring that customers receive assistance whenever they need it.

Consider an e-commerce platform that offers 24/7 customer support through ChatGPT-powered chatbots. A customer, unable to sleep due to a question about their recent purchase, can simply open the website's chat and get an instant response. This level of availability not only increases customer satisfaction but also leads to higher sales as customers feel confident making purchases at any time.

Strategy 6: Seamless Handoffs

While chatbots are excellent at handling routine queries, complex issues often require human intervention. ChatGPT can facilitate seamless handoffs from chatbots to human agents by providing context and relevant information. This ensures a smooth transition and prevents customers from having to repeat themselves when their inquiry escalates.

Imagine a scenario where a customer contacts their internet service provider's chat support regarding a connectivity issue. The chatbot attempts to troubleshoot the problem but realizes it needs further investigation. ChatGPT facilitates the handoff by summarizing the conversation and passing it to a human agent, who can then pick up where the chatbot left off. This ensures that the customer's issue is resolved efficiently and without frustration.

Strategy 7: Issue Resolution

Chatbots can guide customers through troubleshooting processes, helping them resolve common issues on their own. This empowers customers and reduces the workload on your support team. ChatGPT can provide step-by-step instructions, troubleshoot problems, or even offer video tutorials to assist customers in resolving their issues.

Consider a software company that uses ChatGPT-powered virtual assistants to help customers troubleshoot technical problems. When a customer encounters a software glitch, the virtual assistant can walk them through a series of diagnostic steps. If the issue remains unresolved, the virtual assistant can schedule a support call with a human agent, ensuring that the customer's problem is addressed promptly.

Strategy 8: Data Insights

Chatbots can collect and analyze customer data, providing valuable insights into customer preferences, pain points, and common issues. These insights can inform product improvements and marketing strategies, enabling you to make data-driven decisions that enhance both your customer support and overall business.

For instance, an e-commerce platform may use ChatGPT to collect data on customer inquiries and concerns. By analyzing this data, they discover that a significant number of customers have questions about their return policy. Armed with this insight, the company can update its return policy to address common customer concerns, leading to improved customer satisfaction and a reduction in return-related inquiries.

Streamlining Workflows and Improving Satisfaction

Strategy 9: Faster Response Times

In the fast-paced digital age, customers expect quick responses to their inquiries. Chatbots can instantly respond to customer queries, reducing wait times and improving overall satisfaction. Customers appreciate quick and efficient support, which can lead to positive reviews, repeat business, and brand loyalty.

Imagine a telecommunications company using ChatGPT-powered chatbots to handle customer inquiries. When a customer contacts the company with a billing question, the chatbot can provide an immediate response with detailed information about the customer's bill. This not only resolves the customer's issue quickly but also leaves them with a positive impression of the company's responsiveness.

Strategy 10: Consistency

Consistency in customer support is essential for building trust and brand loyalty. Chatbots deliver consistent responses, ensuring that all customers receive the same level of service regardless of the time of day or the support agent they interact with. This consistency builds trust and confidence in your brand.

Consider an online retail platform where customers interact with both chatbots and human agents for support. The chatbots provide consistent and accurate responses to frequently asked questions, ensuring that all customers receive the same information. This consistency fosters trust, as customers know they can rely on the platform for reliable and accurate support.

Strategy 11: Post-Interaction Feedback

Feedback is a valuable tool for improving customer support. Chatbots can solicit feedback from customers after each interaction to gauge their satisfaction and identify areas for improvement. This feedback loop is invaluable for enhancing the quality of customer support and making continuous improvements.

For instance, a customer contacts a travel agency's chat support to inquire about vacation packages. After the interaction, the chatbot asks the customer to rate their experience and provide feedback. The customer provides feedback, expressing their satisfaction with the prompt and helpful responses. The travel agency uses this feedback to recognize the chatbot's effectiveness and can use it as a model for training human support agents.

Case Studies in Customer Support Excellence

To illustrate the power of ChatGPT in enhancing customer support, let's explore a few compelling case studies:

Case Study 1: The E-commerce Giant

An e-commerce giant integrated ChatGPT-powered chatbots into its customer support workflow. These chatbots handled routine queries, such as order tracking and returns. As a result, response times improved significantly, and human agents could focus on resolving complex issues. Customer satisfaction scores soared, leading to increased loyalty and repeat business. The company also used the data collected by the chatbots to identify trends in customer inquiries, allowing them to make targeted improvements to their website and customer support processes.

<u>Case Study 2: The Tech Startup</u>

A tech startup leveraged ChatGPT to provide personalized onboarding assistance to users of its software. Chatbots guided new users through setup and troubleshooting processes, ensuring a smooth onboarding experience. This reduced the burden on the support team and contributed to a higher customer retention rate. The startup also used ChatGPT to offer 24/7 support, making their software more attractive to customers in different time zones.

<u>Case Study 3: The Financial Institution</u>

A financial institution implemented ChatGPT-powered virtual assistants to handle customer inquiries about account balances, transaction history, and common banking procedures. The virtual assistants offered 24/7 support, allowing customers to access their accounts and get answers to their questions at any time.

This convenience translated into improved customer satisfaction and lower support costs. Additionally, the institution used the data collected by the virtual assistants to identify areas where customers needed additional support and launched targeted educational campaigns to address these needs.

Elevating Customer Support with ChatGPT

In this chapter, we've embarked on a journey to elevate customer support through the power of ChatGPT. Exceptional customer support is no longer a luxury but a strategic imperative. By utilizing ChatGPT for personalized experiences, implementing chatbots and virtual assistants, and streamlining workflows, you can enhance customer satisfaction and build lasting relationships with your audience.

Chapter 9: Language Translation and Cross-Cultural Communication

Welcome to another captivating chapter of our journey through the boundless possibilities of ChatGPT. Thus far, we've explored how ChatGPT can revolutionize lead generation, transform marketing content, and elevate customer support. Now, we stand at the crossroads of language and culture, ready to unveil how ChatGPT's language capabilities can transcend linguistic barriers, enabling real-time translation, and fostering a more inclusive global community.

The Tower of Babel: Language as a Barrier

Language, a magnificent gift to humanity, can also be a formidable barrier to effective communication. It possesses the power to convey thoughts, emotions, and ideas, but it can also erect insurmountable walls when individuals and nations lack a common tongue. Misunderstandings, missed opportunities, and even conflicts have historically been rooted in language differences.

But fear not, for ChatGPT is here to shatter these linguistic barriers. This chapter is dedicated to exploring how ChatGPT can help us overcome these obstacles, enabling real-time translation, localization, and creating a more inclusive and connected world.

The Language Alchemist: ChatGPT's Translation Prowess

Strategy 1: Real-time Translation

Imagine a world where you can effortlessly converse with someone from another part of the globe, irrespective of the languages you both speak. This isn't science fiction; it's the power of ChatGPT's real-time translation capabilities.

For instance, consider a scenario where two companies — one based in Japan and the other in France — are engaged in a critical business negotiation. In the past, language barriers might have hindered effective communication. However, with ChatGPT, the conversation flows seamlessly. Each party can speak or type in their native language, and ChatGPT instantaneously translates their words, ensuring that nothing is lost in translation.

Strategy 2: Localization Services

In today's global marketplace, reaching diverse audiences is paramount. Localization— adapting content for different regions and cultures—is the key to success. ChatGPT plays a pivotal role in helping businesses tailor their messaging to resonate with specific audiences, fostering a deeper connection.

Consider an international e-commerce platform seeking to expand its reach in Latin America. ChatGPT assists in translating product descriptions, customer reviews, and marketing materials into Spanish and Portuguese, making the platform more accessible and appealing to the local population. This localization effort leads to increased engagement and sales in the region.

Strategy 3: Breaking Down Language Barriers

Language should never be a barrier to accessing knowledge or participating in discussions. ChatGPT can be harnessed to make educational content, news, and online forums accessible to individuals who speak different languages.

Imagine a global online forum where users discuss a wide range of topics. Language diversity among participants can be a challenge, but ChatGPT acts as an interpreter, translating posts and comments in real time. This ensures that everyone can engage in meaningful discussions and share their insights, regardless of their native language.

Strategy 4: Multilingual Content Creation

Creating content that resonates with a global audience can be a daunting task. ChatGPT, however, excels in generating multilingual content that caters to diverse language preferences.

Consider a multinational corporation launching a global advertising campaign. With ChatGPT's assistance, they can create ad copies, slogans, and marketing materials in multiple languages simultaneously. This not only saves time and resources but also ensures consistency and resonance across different markets.

Bridging Cultures: Enhancing Cross-Cultural Communication

Strategy 5: Cultural Sensitivity

Effective communication transcends mere translation; it requires an understanding of cultural nuances. ChatGPT can be trained to recognize and respect these nuances, avoiding unintended offense and fostering goodwill.

Let's take the example of a travel agency planning to launch a campaign promoting tours to various destinations. ChatGPT, well-versed in cultural intricacies, helps the agency create marketing materials that respect the customs and traditions of each location. This approach ensures that the agency's messaging resonates positively with potential travelers from diverse cultural backgrounds.

Strategy 6: Inclusivity and Accessibility

Inclusivity lies at the core of a harmonious society. ChatGPT can be deployed to make digital content, services, and experiences more accessible to individuals with different language preferences and abilities.

Imagine an educational platform committed to providing free courses to learners worldwide. With ChatGPT's translation capabilities, the platform can offer course materials in multiple languages, breaking down language barriers and opening access to knowledge for individuals who may not have had the opportunity otherwise.

Strategy 7: Promoting Multilingualism

Multilingualism is a valuable asset in our interconnected world. ChatGPT can encourage and support the learning of multiple languages by providing real-time translations and language-learning assistance.

Consider a language learning app that uses ChatGPT to offer immersive language experiences. Users can engage in conversations with ChatGPT in their target language, receiving instant feedback and correction. This interactive approach accelerates language acquisition and encourages users to embrace multilingualism.

Case Studies in Cross-Cultural Communication Excellence

To illustrate the power of ChatGPT in enhancing cross-cultural communication, let's delve into a few captivating case studies:

Case Study 1: The Global Media Conglomerate

A global media conglomerate, with audiences spanning the continents, faced the challenge of making its news articles accessible to readers worldwide. By integrating ChatGPT's translation capabilities into their website, they achieved remarkable results. Readers could instantly translate articles into their preferred language, increasing the publication's global reach and reader engagement. As a bonus, the conglomerate also used ChatGPT to tailor content to different regions, ensuring that articles resonated culturally with local audiences.

Case Study 2: The International NGO

An international non-governmental organization (NGO) focused on humanitarian efforts needed to communicate with diverse communities around the world. With ChatGPT, they broke down language barriers during disaster relief operations. Field workers could communicate with locals, gather critical information, and provide assistance without relying on interpreters. This not only expedited their response but also enhanced the organization's reputation for effective and culturally sensitive aid efforts.

Case Study 3: The Multinational Corporation

A multinational corporation with employees from various cultural backgrounds sought to foster cross-cultural collaboration within its teams. ChatGPT played a pivotal role by assisting in cross-cultural training. It provided employees with instant translations, cultural etiquette guidance, and even facilitated team-building activities that celebrated diversity. This approach not only improved internal communication but also enhanced the company's ability to connect with a global customer base.

Building Bridges with ChatGPT

In this extended chapter, we've embarked on a profound journey through the realm of language translation and cross-cultural communication. We've witnessed how ChatGPT's language capabilities can overcome language barriers, enhance inclusivity, and bridge cultural divides.

As our expedition continues, the next chapter beckons — an exploration of the ethical considerations and responsible use of AI in our ever-evolving world. Join us in the forthcoming chapter as we navigate the intricate landscape of ethics in AI and discover the principles that guide our responsible utilization of this transformative technology. The journey is far from over, and the best is yet to come!

Chapter 10: Research Assistance and Knowledge Exploration

Welcome, esteemed readers, to another enlightening chapter in our journey through the boundless capabilities of ChatGPT. In this extended exploration, we will delve deep into the multifaceted ways in which ChatGPT, armed with its vast knowledge base, can redefine the landscape of research, maximize efficiency, and kindle the flames of innovation in domains as diverse as academia, journalism, and beyond.

The Pursuit of Knowledge

The pursuit of knowledge has, for centuries, been the driving force behind human progress. It is the relentless quest for understanding, the unwavering commitment to uncovering truths, and the insatiable hunger for enlightenment. Whether one is a scientist seeking to decipher the secrets of the cosmos, a journalist dedicated to exposing hidden truths, or a scholar diving into the depths of academia, the pursuit of knowledge is a timeless endeavor. However, this journey can often be fraught with challenges—an ocean of data, labyrinthine archives, and an overwhelming deluge of information.

Enter ChatGPT, a beacon of knowledge and an unwavering ally in your quest for answers. This chapter is dedicated to illuminating the myriad ways in which ChatGPT can serve as your guiding star through the labyrinth of research, making data analysis, information gathering, and fact-checking not only more efficient but also more profound.

The Scholar's Emissary: ChatGPT's Vast Knowledge Base

Strategy 1: Illuminating Literature Reviews

For scholars and researchers, embarking on a comprehensive literature review is often the first step in any research expedition. It is the process of immersing oneself in the existing body of research and publications related to one's field, providing the intellectual bedrock upon which new discoveries are built. Traditionally, this endeavor demands hours of painstakingly sifting through academic journals, books, and articles.

With ChatGPT as your scholarly companion, this arduous journey transforms into a swift and enlightening expedition. Envision a doctoral student setting sail on a literature review for their dissertation in the field of astrophysics. Instead of drowning in a sea of papers, they form an alliance with ChatGPT to generate concise summaries, pinpoint key insights, and even receive critical analytical perspectives. ChatGPT's efficiency and formidable knowledge base expedite the review process, allowing the student to ascend to more advanced research pursuits with newfound clarity and purpose.

Strategy 2: Data Analysis and Interpretation Amplified

In domains such as data science and business analytics, the ability to deftly analyze and interpret data is the keystone of success. Researchers and analysts are often confronted with vast datasets, intricate statistical models, and the pressing need for rapid insights.

ChatGPT stands ready as a versatile ally in this arena. Envision a data analyst tasked with delving into a colossal dataset brimming with customer behavior metrics. ChatGPT takes on the mantle of a data virtuoso, assisting in the creation of data visualizations, generating succinct statistical summaries, and even formulating hypotheses grounded in the intricate patterns of data. By forging an alliance with ChatGPT, the analyst not only expedites the analysis but also unearths profound insights that might have otherwise remained concealed in the labyrinthine depths of data.

Strategy 3: Veracious Information Gathering and Fact-Checking

Journalists and writers are the vanguards of truth in an era inundated with information. Their craft hinges on the veracity of their sources and the credibility of their narratives. In a world where disinformation and misinformation abound, the critical task of distinguishing fact from fiction has become more formidable than ever.

ChatGPT emerges as a trusted companion in the arena of fact-checking and information gathering. Picture an investigative journalist embarking on an unrelenting quest to uncover a network of corrupt officials entangled in a web of deceit. The trail of deceit led to a multitude of sources, each concealing fragments of the truth. With ChatGPT as their truth-seeking companion, the journalist delves deep into the labyrinth of information. ChatGPT meticulously cross-references sources, discerns credible references from dubious ones, and unfailingly flags inconsistencies for further scrutiny. This rigorous fact-checking regimen ensures that the final piece not only bears the mantle of credibility but also upholds the sacred tenets of ethical journalism, illuminating the truth in the darkest corners of society.

Strategy 4: Catalyzing Collaborative Innovation

Innovation, the lifeblood of progress, often thrives in the fertile soil of collaboration — where diverse minds converge, ideas intertwine, and groundbreaking solutions emerge. ChatGPT, armed with its boundless knowledge, becomes a potent catalyst for creative thinking and problem-solving.

Imagine a team of engineers setting forth on a grand quest to revolutionize the field of sustainable energy. Their mission is to unlock the secrets of renewable power generation and storage. In this quest, they enlist ChatGPT as their trusted ally. ChatGPT immerses itself in the latest research papers, swiftly distilling complex energy concepts into comprehensible insights. During brainstorming sessions, ChatGPT contributes innovative ideas based on emerging trends in renewable energy. This collaborative synergy sets the stage for a transformative journey of innovation. The startup unveiled a revolutionary genetic sequencing technology that promised to transform the field of personalized medicine, offering new hope to patients worldwide.

Case Studies in Knowledge Exploration Excellence

To illuminate the transformative power of ChatGPT in research assistance and knowledge exploration, let us embark on an enthralling voyage through a series of captivating case studies:

Case Study 1: The Scientific Odyssey

A team of brilliant scientists, nestled in the heart of a renowned research institution, embarked on a grand scientific odyssey. Their quest was to unravel the mysteries of quantum physics — the enigmatic realm where particles behave in baffling ways. Their journey led them into the labyrinthine corridors of academic literature, where complex theories and elusive discoveries lay buried. Leveraging ChatGPT's prowess, they embarked on an expedition through the annals of quantum physics literature. ChatGPT served as their astute guide, meticulously summarizing seminal papers, pinpointing crucial equations, and providing clarity on the most enigmatic theories. This collaboration with ChatGPT culminated in a groundbreaking paper that not only advanced our understanding of quantum mechanics but also earned the team accolades on the global stage, propelling them to the forefront of scientific discovery.

Case Study 2: The Investigative Chronicle

In the world of journalism, where the pursuit of truth is paramount, an investigative journalist took on the mantle of an intrepid truth-seeker. Their mission was to expose a clandestine network of corrupt politicians, ensnared in a web of intrigue. The trail of deceit led to a multitude of sources, each concealing fragments of the truth. With ChatGPT as their unwavering companion, the journalist embarked on a relentless quest for veracity. ChatGPT meticulously cross-referenced sources, analyzed financial records, and highlighted incongruities in the narratives of the accused. This tireless fact-checking partnership resulted in a series of revelatory exposés that not only rocked the foundations of political corruption but also ignited a public outcry for justice, reaffirming the role of journalism as a beacon of accountability.

Case Study 3: The Innovation Odyssey

In the realm of biotechnology, a dynamic startup set its sights on pioneering breakthroughs in genomics. Their vision was to decode the secrets of the human genome and unlock the potential for personalized medicine. To navigate the intricate landscape of genetic research, they called upon ChatGPT as their research vanguard. ChatGPT immersed itself in the latest research papers, swiftly distilling complex genetic concepts into comprehensible insights. During brainstorming sessions, ChatGPT contributed innovative ideas based on emerging trends in genomics. This collaborative synergy set the stage for a transformative journey of innovation. The startup unveiled a revolutionary genetic sequencing technology that promised to transform the field of personalized medicine, offering new hope to patients worldwide.

Charting New Frontiers with ChatGPT

In this extended and illuminating chapter, we've embarked on an exhilarating odyssey through the realm of research assistance and knowledge exploration. We've witnessed how ChatGPT, armed with its boundless knowledge base, expedites literature reviews, enhances data analysis, ensures the veracity of information, and catalyzes collaborative innovation.

As our expedition continues, let us pause to reflect upon the profound implications of ChatGPT's capabilities. It has illuminated new pathways across diverse domains, unraveling the mysteries of the universe, unveiling the hidden truths of society, and propelling innovation to unprecedented heights.

In the chapters that follow, we shall delve into the overarching ethical considerations that accompany the integration of ChatGPT into our lives. Together, we shall navigate the intricate landscape of ethics in AI, forging principles that will guide our judicious and responsible utilization of this transformative technology. The journey is far from over, and the best is yet to come—an era where knowledge knows no bounds, and innovation knows no limits.

Chapter 11: Unleashing the Revenue Potential of ChatGPT as Your Virtual Assistant

In an age of unparalleled technological advancement, where the limits of income generation continually expand, ChatGPT emerges as a trailblazer in the realm of virtual assistance. In this extensive exploration, we will embark on a thrilling journey, uncovering how ChatGPT, the remarkable AI marvel, can elevate your productivity while also becoming a dynamic source of income. Imagine having an unflinching, efficient, and ever-ready virtual assistant, capable of managing an array of tasks with finesse and precision. The opportunities that this collaboration presents are as vast as ChatGPT's potential, and together, we will dive deep into this sea of possibilities.

The Evolution of Virtual Assistance

Before we plunge into the exhilarating prospects that ChatGPT offers as a virtual assistant, let's take a moment to appreciate the profound shift in our work culture. Gone are the days when virtual assistants were solely human beings constrained by time zones and human limitations. Today, AI-driven virtual assistants like ChatGPT herald a new era of virtual assistance — one marked by unmatched efficiency, accessibility, and scalability.

Whether you're an entrepreneur striving to streamline operations, a professional yearning to declutter your schedule, or an individual seeking to regain control of your life, ChatGPT stands ready to assist. The opportunities that ChatGPT offers as a virtual assistant are boundless. Let's embark on this journey to discover how you can transform ChatGPT's capabilities into sources of income.

Opportunity 1: Scheduling and Calendar Mastery

Envision the life of a CEO, a whirlwind of meetings, appointments, and deadlines. This is where ChatGPT steps in as the unwavering virtual assistant. It doesn't just schedule appointments with pinpoint precision but also dispatches timely reminders, ensuring that no commitment falls through the cracks.

Case Study: The Busy CEO's Secret Weapon

Meet Sarah, the CEO of a thriving tech startup. Her daily routine is a complex web of meetings with investors, product launches, and strategic planning sessions. The weight of her responsibilities could easily overwhelm her, jeopardizing her efficiency.

In her quest for optimal efficiency, she enlists ChatGPT as her virtual assistant. ChatGPT takes charge of her calendar, skillfully navigating the intricate web of appointments, coordinating with stakeholders, and even drafting email invitations with diplomatic finesse. The result? Sarah's life becomes more organized, and she can devote her time and energy to growing her business rather than micro-managing her schedule. Recognizing the remarkable time and stress-saving benefits of ChatGPT's assistance, Sarah decides to extend ChatGPT's scheduling services to fellow entrepreneurs. The demand for such services skyrockets, swiftly establishing a lucrative and steady income stream.

Opportunity 2: Tailored Task Management

In a world brimming with tasks and to-do lists, staying organized can be a Herculean task. This is where ChatGPT shines as a virtual assistant par excellence. It aids individuals and professionals alike in managing their tasks, creating to-do lists, and prioritizing responsibilities.

Case Study: The Freelancer's Champion

Meet Alex, a freelance graphic designer. His life is a whirlwind of client projects, deadlines, and creative pursuits. As his workload escalates, he finds himself struggling to keep track of commitments and maintain organizational clarity. The resulting chaos threatens to sap his productivity and jeopardize his client relationships.

In this time of need, Alex turns to ChatGPT as his virtual assistant. ChatGPT not only creates a comprehensive task management system but also offers guidance on prioritizing assignments based on deadlines and importance. It even suggests optimal work hours, tailored to Alex's unique productivity patterns. With ChatGPT's assistance, Alex experiences a significant surge in efficiency and productivity. Impressed by the transformative results, Alex decides to extend ChatGPT's task management services to fellow freelancers. As word spreads about the incredible organizational skills of his AI-powered virtual assistant, Alex's income from this endeavor surpasses his initial expectations.

Opportunity 3: Multilingual Communication and Language Mastery

In an increasingly globalized world, the ability to communicate in multiple languages is a coveted skill. ChatGPT, with its language capabilities, can serve as an invaluable virtual assistant for translation, fostering cross-cultural communication with ease.

Case Study: The Global PR Luminary

Meet Elena, a public relations specialist with a client base spanning continents. Her clients demand a high level of precision and cultural sensitivity in their communication. Each project necessitates the translation of press releases, marketing materials, and emails into multiple languages, ensuring that her clients' messages resonate with their target audiences.

Elena employs ChatGPT as her virtual language assistant. ChatGPT deftly translates content into various languages while preserving the nuance and tone of the original message. This not only saves Elena a substantial amount of time but also elevates the quality of her work.

As word spreads about Elena's ability to provide top-tier multilingual communication services, her client base grows, and so does her income. She decides to expand her PR agency's services to include ChatGPT's language translation expertise, unlocking a lucrative revenue stream. ChatGPT's assistance not only amplifies her efficiency but also broadens the horizons of her business.

Opportunity 4: Content Creation and Social Media Mastery

In the digital age, content is the currency of influence, and maintaining a robust online presence is imperative. ChatGPT, with its exceptional writing skills and social media acumen, can be the ultimate virtual assistant for content creation and management.

Case Study: The Influencer's Right Hand

Meet Jake, a budding social media influencer determined to grow his online presence. His meteoric rise to stardom relies on captivating content that captivates his followers. However, the demands of consistently producing high-quality content and managing his social media accounts are becoming increasingly challenging.

Enter ChatGPT, his virtual assistant and secret weapon. ChatGPT not only generates captivating blog posts, tweets, and Instagram captions but also tailors them to Jake's unique style and personality. The AI virtual assistant manages his social media accounts adeptly, posting content at optimal times, responding to comments, and analyzing engagement data.

With ChatGPT's assistance, Jake's following grows exponentially, and brands clamor to collaborate with him. Recognizing the potential, Jake extends ChatGPT's content creation and social media management services to fellow influencers. This diversifies his income streams, solidifying his status as an influencer powerhouse.

Monetizing Virtual Assistance: Strategies and Insights

Now, let's delve into the art of monetizing this exceptional virtual assistance service. The income generation possibilities are as diverse as the tasks ChatGPT can undertake. Here are some strategies, each with insights on setting them up:

- Subscription-Based Model
  - This model involves offering access to ChatGPT's virtual assistance services on a subscription basis.
  - Users pay a recurring monthly or annual fee to access the AI-powered assistance.

- o This model ensures a steady stream of income as long as you provide valuable assistance.
- o To implement a subscription-based model, create tiers of subscription plans that cater to different needs.
- o For example, you can offer a basic plan with essential services and a premium plan with more advanced features.
- o Consider offering a free trial to entice potential subscribers.
- Per-Task Arrangements
  - o In this approach, users pay for specific tasks or services provided by ChatGPT.
  - o This offers flexibility, allowing users to pay only for the services they require, making it a cost-effective option.
  - o Define a clear pricing structure for various tasks or services.
  - o Ensure transparency in pricing to build trust with your clients.
  - o Implement a user-friendly system for requesting and paying for tasks, such as a dedicated website or app.

- Package Deals
  - Create customized packages that bundle multiple virtual assistant services together.
  - For instance, offer a "Productivity Powerhouse" package that includes scheduling, task management, and content creation.
  - These packages can be priced competitively, encouraging users to opt for comprehensive assistance.
  - Design attractive package deals that cater to different customer segments.
  - Promote these packages as cost-effective solutions for clients seeking a comprehensive virtual assistant experience.
  - Create clear package descriptions and pricing tiers.
- Affiliate Partnerships
  - Explore partnerships with businesses or platforms that complement ChatGPT's services.
  - You can earn a commission for referring users or businesses to

these partners, expanding your income potential.

- o Identify potential partners whose services align with ChatGPT's offerings.
- o Establish affiliate agreements and track referrals using specialized software or platforms.
- o Promote these partnerships to your user base.
- Training and Consultation
  - o Position yourself as an expert in leveraging ChatGPT's capabilities.
  - o Offer training sessions or consultation services to individuals or businesses looking to maximize their use of ChatGPT.
  - o Develop training materials and modules that cover various aspects of ChatGPT's functionality.
  - o Host webinars, workshops, or one-on-one consultations.
  - o Promote your expertise through your website and marketing efforts.

A Wealth of Possibilities

In this comprehensive exploration, we've navigated the exhilarating realm of income generation with ChatGPT as a virtual assistant. From scheduling and task management to language translation and content creation, the opportunities are boundless. Whether you're an entrepreneur looking to streamline operations or an individual seeking to regain control of your life, ChatGPT is the virtual assistant you've been waiting for.

Remember, success lies not only in utilizing ChatGPT's virtual assistance but also in exploring innovative ways to monetize these services. Subscription models, per-task arrangements, package deals, affiliate partnerships, and expert training are just the beginning.

As we continue our journey of income generation with ChatGPT, we'll uncover additional opportunities, strategies, and case studies that will inspire you to unlock the full potential of this AI marvel. Stay tuned, for the adventure has just begun, and the horizon of possibilities stretches as far as your imagination can reach.

Chapter 12: Monetizing Knowledge and Expertise with ChatGPT-Powered Online Courses

In our rapidly evolving digital landscape, the traditional boundaries of education are undergoing a profound transformation. With the advent of AI technologies like ChatGPT, the realm of online education is poised to revolutionize how we acquire knowledge and expertise. In this chapter, we will embark on a journey to explore the vast opportunities that ChatGPT presents for creating, delivering, and monetizing engaging online courses. It's not just about sharing knowledge; it's about empowering learners and unlocking new income streams.

The Paradigm Shift in Education

Before we delve into the exciting realm of ChatGPT-powered online courses, it's essential to acknowledge the seismic shifts reshaping education. Gone are the days when learning was confined to the physical classroom. Today, learners seek flexible, personalized, and interactive educational experiences that adapt to their unique needs and schedules.

ChatGPT, with its natural language processing and conversation capabilities, represents a giant leap forward in making education more engaging and accessible. With its assistance, educators and experts can craft learning experiences that cater to diverse learners worldwide. Let's explore how you can leverage ChatGPT to tap into this transformative landscape and monetize your knowledge and expertise.

Opportunity 1: Crafting Immersive and Interactive Courses

Imagine an online course that's not a static collection of videos and text but a dynamic, conversational learning experience. ChatGPT can serve as your virtual teaching assistant, facilitating discussions, answering questions, and providing real-time feedback.

Case Study: The Language Learning Revolution

Meet Dr. Elena, a language enthusiast passionate about helping others become fluent in multiple languages. In the past, she relied on traditional teaching methods and pre-recorded video lessons. However, she felt that language learning should be more interactive and engaging.

Elena decides to employ ChatGPT as her teaching assistant. She creates an online language course where ChatGPT acts as a virtual conversation partner for learners. They practice speaking and listening skills by conversing with ChatGPT, which provides instant feedback, pronunciation tips, and suggestions for improvement. The result? Elena's course becomes a sensation in the language learning community. Learners rave about the immersive experience, and word-of-mouth spreads like wildfire. The course's popularity translates into substantial revenue for Elena, who is now considering expanding into other languages and topics.

Monetization Potential: Elena's language learning course has over 10,000 enrolled learners, with each course priced at $99. With a 50% profit margin, she has earned $495,000 in revenue. The word-of-mouth marketing, she employs helps her acquire new learners continuously, potentially increasing her income exponentially.

Opportunity 2: Personalized Learning at Scale

One-size-fits-all education is a thing of the past. Today's learners have diverse backgrounds, goals, and learning paces.

ChatGPT can tailor learning experiences to individual needs, adapting content, pacing, and assessments accordingly.

Case Study: The Personalized Math Tutor

Meet Professor John, a mathematics educator who understands that students learn at different rates. Some students need extra practice, while others require advanced challenges. John decides to use ChatGPT to create a personalized math tutoring platform.

Each student interacts with ChatGPT, which assesses their current proficiency and adapts lessons accordingly. If a student struggles with algebra, ChatGPT provides additional exercises and explanations. If another student excels, ChatGPT presents advanced problems to keep them engaged.

Parents and students are thrilled with the results. Test scores rise, and the personalized approach makes learning math a rewarding experience. John monetizes his platform by offering subscription-based access to the personalized tutoring service. As the word spreads about the incredible progress students are making, the platform's user base expands, and John's income soars.

Monetization Potential: John's personalized math tutoring platform has 2,000 subscribers paying $30 per month. This results in monthly revenue of $60,000. After accounting for platform maintenance and ChatGPT's licensing fees, John enjoys a monthly profit of $40,000.

Opportunity 3: Monetizing Your Expertise

If you possess specialized knowledge or skills, ChatGPT can help you monetize your expertise by creating tutorials, guides, or entire courses for a niche audience eager to learn from you.

Case Study: The Artisanal Coffee Connoisseur

Meet Mark, a coffee connoisseur with an encyclopedic knowledge of coffee beans, roasting techniques, and brewing methods. His passion is infectious, and friends often seek his guidance to elevate their coffee experiences. Mark decides to turn his passion into a lucrative venture.

With ChatGPT's assistance, Mark creates an online coffee academy. The academy offers courses on everything from bean selection to latte art. ChatGPT serves as the course facilitator, answering questions, providing detailed explanations, and even conducting virtual taste tests.

Coffee enthusiasts worldwide flock to Mark's academy. They appreciate the personalized guidance and the opportunity to interact with an expert. Mark monetizes his academy through course fees, premium memberships, and exclusive coffee bean subscriptions. As the academy gains recognition, Mark's income grows, and he becomes a recognized authority in the coffee world.

Monetization Potential: Mark's coffee academy has 5,000 registered members. With an average annual membership fee of $199 and additional revenue from one-time course purchases and premium subscriptions, Mark's total annual revenue surpasses $1 million.

Monetizing Your Educational Initiatives

Creating ChatGPT-powered online courses is an exciting venture, but the key lies in turning it into a sustainable source of income. Let's explore strategies for monetizing your educational endeavors:

Course Sales

This straightforward approach involves selling individual courses or course bundles. Learners pay a one-time fee to access your content. To succeed:

- Choose a Platform: Select a platform or website to host your courses. Popular choices include Udemy, Teachable, and Thinkific.
- Invest in Quality: Produce high-quality content, including videos, interactive elements, and well-designed materials.
- Promote Aggressively: Market your courses through social media, email marketing, and collaborations with influencers or educational platforms.

Monetization Potential: Suppose you sell a course priced at $149, and 1,000 learners purchase it. This results in $149,000 in revenue, assuming a 100% profit margin.

Membership Models

Consider offering subscription-based memberships that provide access to a library of courses or ongoing educational content. Subscribers pay a monthly or annual fee for continuous learning. To make this work:

- Content Schedule: Develop a content release schedule to keep members engaged and ensure they receive ongoing value.
- User-Friendly Platform: Create a user-friendly platform where members can

easily access courses, track progress, and engage with ChatGPT.

Monetization Potential: If you have 500 subscribers paying $25 per month, you generate $12,500 in monthly recurring revenue. Over a year, that's $150,000 in revenue.

Premium Content and Exclusive Access

Offer premium content, such as advanced courses or personalized coaching sessions, at a higher price point. This appeals to learners looking for deeper knowledge or one-on-one guidance. Here's how:

- Clearly Define Premium Offerings: Make sure your premium offerings are well-defined, highlighting the additional value they provide.
- Marketing Strategy: Promote these premium options to your existing user base and potential customers, emphasizing the unique benefits they offer.

Monetization Potential: Suppose you offer premium coaching sessions at $150 per hour, and you book 20 hours of coaching per month. This results in $36,000 in annual revenue from coaching alone.

Affiliate Marketing

Partner with educational platforms or websites and earn a commission for referring learners to their courses. This strategy can complement your own course offerings and diversify your income sources. Here's how to set it up:

- Identify Partners: Identify reputable educational platforms or products that align with your content.
- Join Affiliate Programs: Sign up for their affiliate programs and incorporate affiliate links or promotions within your courses or tutorials.
- Transparent Recommendations: Ensure transparency and provide genuine recommendations to build trust with your audience.

Monetization Potential: If you earn a 30% commission for each successful referral and you refer 100 learners to a $100 course, you generate $3,000 in affiliate income.

Consulting and Coaching Services

Leverage your expertise to offer consulting or coaching services to learners seeking personalized guidance. Charge an hourly or session-based fee for one-on-one interactions. Here's how to get started:

- Professional Profile: Create a professional consulting or coaching profile on platforms like LinkedIn or specialized coaching websites.
- Promote Services: Advertise your services within your educational content and invite interested learners to book sessions.
- Build a Reputation: Provide exceptional value during sessions to build a positive reputation and generate word-of-mouth referrals.

Monetization Potential: If you offer consulting services at $100 per hour and you book 10 hours of consulting per week, you generate $5,200 in monthly consulting income.

Realizing the Income Potential

As we've explored, the income potential of ChatGPT-powered online courses and educational initiatives is substantial. The exact figures will depend on factors such as the quality of your content, your marketing efforts, and your ability to engage your audience. However, it's crucial to note that the income generated can be substantial and potentially even surpass traditional income sources.

The stories of Dr. Elena, Professor John, and Mark demonstrate how individuals with diverse expertise can leverage ChatGPT to monetize their knowledge effectively. These case studies exemplify the possibilities, but they're just the tip of the iceberg. The world is hungry for knowledge and expertise, and ChatGPT has opened the door for educators and experts to meet this demand while creating a lucrative income stream.

The Future of Education and Income Generation

In this transformative age of education, ChatGPT serves as a beacon of innovation, guiding us toward new possibilities in learning and income generation. The ability to create interactive, personalized, and monetizable online courses is within your reach.

As we conclude this chapter, remember that education isn't just about imparting knowledge; it's also about empowering others to reach their full potential. By harnessing ChatGPT's capabilities, you can shape the future of education while building a rewarding source of income. The journey of discovery and learning never ends, and ChatGPT is your faithful companion on this exciting path of educational entrepreneurship. Your income potential is limited only by your creativity, dedication, and commitment to delivering value to your learners. The future of education is here, and it's incredibly bright.

Chapter 13: Elevating Game Development and Interactive Storytelling with ChatGPT

Welcome to a world where pixels meet imagination, where lines of code transform into immersive adventures, and where ChatGPT takes center stage in the enchanting realm of game development and interactive storytelling. In this extended chapter, we'll embark on a journey through the captivating landscapes of gaming, exploring the profound influence ChatGPT wields in creating engaging narratives, crafting interactive characters, building immersive experiences, and monetizing your gaming creations. Get ready for an odyssey where players aren't just spectators; they're active participants in stories that come alive before their eyes.

The Evolution of Gaming and Storytelling

Before we dive into the exhilarating possibilities ChatGPT brings to the gaming world, let's take a moment to appreciate the evolution of storytelling in games. Gone are the days of linear narratives where players passively watched events unfold. Modern gaming invites players to shape the story, make crucial decisions, and interact with characters who respond dynamically.

ChatGPT takes this evolution to new heights. Its natural language processing abilities enable it to understand and generate human-like text, making interactions with virtual characters feel more genuine and engaging. Let's explore how ChatGPT's integration into game development can revolutionize storytelling.

Opportunity 1: Enhancing Game Narratives

Imagine playing a game where the story adapts to your choices, and the characters respond in a lifelike manner. ChatGPT's ability to generate dynamic dialogues and adapt to player decisions can elevate game narratives to unprecedented levels of immersion.

Case Study: "The Odyssey Reimagined"

Meet Jane, an independent game developer with a passion for classical literature. She decides to create a game based on Homer's epic, "The Odyssey," where players take on the role of Odysseus. In her game, ChatGPT powers the character interactions.

As players navigate the challenges Odysseus faces, they engage in conversations with gods, mythical creatures, and fellow travelers. ChatGPT ensures that every interaction feels unique and tailored to the player's choices. Depending on players' decisions, the story unfolds in various directions, offering multiple endings.

"The Odyssey Reimagined" captivates players with its immersive storytelling. Each decision they make affects the narrative, and they feel emotionally connected to the characters. Jane monetizes her game through in-game purchases, offering cosmetic items and additional story chapters, resulting in substantial revenue.

Monetization Potential: Suppose Jane sells her game for $29.99, and 100,000 players purchase it. This results in $2,999,000 in revenue. Additionally, in-game purchases can add another $500,000 in revenue over the game's lifespan.

Opportunity 2: Creating Interactive Characters

In the gaming world, characters are the heart and soul of the experience. ChatGPT empowers developers to create interactive characters that players can truly connect with.

Case Study: "The Cyber Detective"

Imagine a futuristic detective game set in a sprawling, cyberpunk city. In this game, players collaborate with an AI-driven partner, a cyber detective named Vega. Vega is not a pre-programmed character; she's powered by ChatGPT, enabling real-time conversations and adaptive responses.

Players work with Vega to solve intricate cases, gather information, and make choices that affect the game's outcome. Vega's conversational abilities make her a dynamic partner who adapts to players' playstyles and choices. Her witty remarks, emotional support, and evolving personality create a strong bond between players and their virtual partner.

"The Cyber Detective" offers both a free version with ads and a premium version without ads. Many players choose the premium version to enjoy an uninterrupted gaming experience and deepen their connection with Vega, resulting in a steady stream of revenue.

Monetization Potential: If 5% of players opt for the premium version at $4.99 and the game has 500,000 downloads, this results in $124,750 in revenue. Additionally, in-game advertisements can generate an extra $50,000 over time.

Opportunity 3: Crafting Immersive Experiences

Immersive storytelling is not just about dialogue; it's about creating worlds that players can lose themselves in. ChatGPT's capabilities extend to generating rich descriptions, environmental storytelling, and guiding players through intricate game worlds.

<u>Case Study: "Mystic Realms Online"</u>

Enter the enchanting world of "Mystic Realms Online," a massive multiplayer online role-playing game (MMORPG) where players explore a vast, magical realm. ChatGPT plays a crucial role in creating the game's immersive experience.

As players traverse forests, ancient ruins, and mystical cities, ChatGPT generates descriptive narratives that breathe life into the game world. Whether it's the rustling of leaves in the wind or the intricate carvings on an ancient artifact, ChatGPT ensures that players are fully immersed in their surroundings.

Additionally, ChatGPT assists players by providing hints, lore, and guidance through quests. It adapts to players' preferences, offering help when needed but never spoiling the sense of discovery.

"Mystic Realms Online" employs a free-to-play model with in-game purchases. Players can buy cosmetic items, mounts, and premium access to new content. The immersive world, enhanced by ChatGPT's contributions, keeps players engaged and willing to invest in the game.

Monetization Potential: With 1,000,000 downloads, "Mystic Realms Online" generates substantial revenue from in-game purchases, easily surpassing $1,000,000 in revenue within the first year.

Monetizing Your Gaming Creations

Creating immersive games with ChatGPT is exhilarating, but to sustain your development efforts and turn your passion into a profitable venture, monetization is key. Let's explore strategies for monetizing your gaming creations:

In-Game Purchases

Offer players the option to purchase cosmetic items, character upgrades, or additional story chapters within your game. Ensure these purchases enhance the player's experience without creating a pay-to-win scenario.

Monetization Potential: Suppose your game has 100,000 players, and 10% of them make an average in-game purchase of $10. This results in $100,000 in revenue.

Subscription Models

Introduce subscription-based models that grant players access to exclusive content, in-game perks, or an ad-free experience. Monthly or annual subscription options can provide a steady income stream.

Monetization Potential: If you have 5,000 subscribers paying $5 per month, you generate $25,000 in monthly recurring revenue.

In-Game Advertising

Incorporate non-intrusive in-game advertisements or sponsorships. Ensure ads are relevant to your player demographic and seamlessly integrated into the game world.

Monetization Potential: Depending on ad impressions and click-through rates, you can earn a significant income, especially if your game has a large player base.

Crowdfunding and Early Access

Engage with your community by offering crowdfunding campaigns or early access to your game. This not only generates funds but also builds a dedicated player base.

Monetization Potential: A successful crowdfunding campaign can yield thousands or even millions of dollars, depending on your game's appeal and marketing efforts.

Merchandising and Licensing

Explore opportunities to license your game's characters or intellectual property for merchandise, such as clothing, toys, or collectibles.

Monetization Potential: Licensing agreements can result in ongoing royalty payments, creating a passive income stream.

Crafting Interactive Adventures

As we conclude this extended chapter, remember that the fusion of ChatGPT and game development opens doors to crafting interactive adventures that captivate players on an unprecedented level. Whether you're creating epic narratives, interactive characters, or immersive worlds, ChatGPT is your creative ally.

The gaming industry is a dynamic, ever-expanding realm filled with opportunities for storytellers, designers, and developers. With ChatGPT's assistance, you have the power to create experiences that resonate with players, keep them engaged, and generate revenue streams that reward your creativity.

The future of gaming and interactive storytelling is limited only by your imagination. As technology continues to evolve, so do the possibilities. ChatGPT is your passport to this exciting world where stories come to life, and players become the heroes of their own adventures. So, pick up your virtual pen and embark on your journey to crafting unforgettable gaming experiences, where the only limit is the boundless realm of your imagination.

Chapter 14: The Power of ChatGPT in Digital Consultancy Services

In the ever-shifting sands of the digital landscape, businesses and individuals are faced with a constant barrage of questions, challenges, and opportunities. Navigating this complex terrain often requires guidance from experts who can provide insights, advice, and solutions. However, in this age of artificial intelligence, a new kind of consultancy service is emerging—one that harnesses the extraordinary capabilities of ChatGPT to offer specialized expertise, personalized recommendations, and effective problem-solving. In this chapter, we will take a deep dive into how ChatGPT can be leveraged to provide digital consultancy services that not only transform businesses but also create a lucrative income stream for savvy entrepreneurs.

The Digital Consultancy Revolution

Traditional consultancy services have long been the trusted advisors of businesses and individuals seeking guidance in various domains. These experts offer a wealth of knowledge and experience to help clients make informed decisions. However, the dawn of the digital age has ushered in a profound transformation. In an era where data, technology, and innovation reign supreme, traditional consultancies are being complemented — and sometimes even replaced — by digital consultancy services. These services, powered by ChatGPT, offer a multitude of advantages:

- Instant Access to Expertise
  - ChatGPT can swiftly access vast repositories of information and stay updated with the latest trends, allowing it to provide insights and solutions in real-time.
- Personalization
  - By understanding the unique needs and context of each client, ChatGPT can deliver tailored advice and recommendations.
- Cost-Efficiency
  - Digital consultancy services powered by ChatGPT can often be more cost-effective than hiring human consultants, particularly for small and medium-sized businesses and startups.

This transformation in the consultancy landscape presents a remarkable opportunity for entrepreneurs and professionals to harness the potential of ChatGPT and offer invaluable guidance in an increasingly digital world.

Opportunity 1: Specialized Consulting Services

One of the most compelling aspects of ChatGPT is its versatility. It can serve as a digital consultant across a wide array of specialized fields, from marketing and finance to technology and healthcare. Let's delve into a real-world example:

Case Study: Marketing Maven

Meet Sarah, a seasoned marketing professional with years of experience working for Fortune 500 companies. Recognizing the growing demand for digital marketing expertise among small businesses, she decides to launch a digital consultancy service with a focus on helping these enterprises improve their online presence and reach. ChatGPT becomes her trusted partner in delivering specialized services.

Small business owners like Mike, who runs a quaint local bakery, seek Sarah's guidance. They want to understand how to harness the power of digital marketing to attract more customers. Sarah's ChatGPT-powered consultancy service provides personalized advice that is tailored to each business's unique needs and budget. Mike receives a comprehensive digital marketing plan, including recommendations on social media strategies, content creation, and search engine optimization.

Sarah monetizes her consultancy service through retainer fees, where clients pay a monthly fee for ongoing advice and support. The accessibility of ChatGPT allows her to efficiently serve multiple clients simultaneously.

Monetization Potential: Sarah charges clients a retainer fee of $1,000 per month. With 20 clients, she generates $20,000 in monthly revenue.

Opportunity 2: Personalized Advice and Recommendations

One of ChatGPT's standout features is its ability to provide personalized advice and recommendations. This personal touch can be a game-changer in consultancy services.

Case Study: Financial Guru

Imagine Tom, a financial consultant who assists individuals in managing their investments and planning for retirement. To enhance the quality of his services, he integrates ChatGPT into his consultancy.

Clients like Lisa, who is diligently saving for retirement, rely on Tom's expertise. With ChatGPT's assistance, Tom crafts investment portfolios tailored to each client's financial goals, risk tolerance, and time horizon. Lisa receives a comprehensive investment plan, complete with asset allocation recommendations and periodic portfolio adjustments.

Tom charges clients a fee based on the assets he manages, ensuring that his success is aligned with theirs.

Monetization Potential: If Tom manages assets worth $5 million for his clients and charges an annual fee of 1%, he generates $50,000 in annual revenue.

Opportunity 3: Problem Solving and Decision Support

In the ever-evolving business landscape, decision-makers often encounter intricate problems that demand innovative solutions.

ChatGPT can serve as a reliable partner in problem-solving.

Case Study: Tech Innovator

Consider Mark, an entrepreneur in the technology sector. He runs a startup that develops cutting-edge AI applications. When his team encounters technical challenges, Mark turns to ChatGPT for problem-solving.

With ChatGPT's assistance, Mark's team tackles issues such as optimizing algorithms, improving user interfaces, and troubleshooting software bugs. ChatGPT provides detailed insights, code snippets, and suggestions for overcoming hurdles. Mark's startup benefits from faster problem resolution and increased productivity.

Mark recognizes an opportunity to offer ChatGPT-powered consultancy services to other tech startups facing similar challenges. He monetizes these services through project-based contracts, where clients pay for specific problem-solving tasks.

Monetization Potential: Mark charges $2,500 per project, and he completes an average of 10 projects per month, resulting in $25,000 in monthly revenue.

Monetizing Your Consultancy Services

Now that we've explored the diverse opportunities for offering digital consultancy services powered by ChatGPT, let's discuss strategies for monetization:

Retainer Fees

Charge clients a monthly or annual retainer fee for ongoing access to your consultancy services. This model ensures a steady stream of income while providing clients with continuous support and advice.

Monetization Potential: If you have 30 clients paying a monthly retainer fee of $1,500, you generate $45,000 in monthly recurring revenue.

Hourly Rates

Offer your services on an hourly basis, especially if clients require occasional assistance or project-specific guidance. Determine your hourly rate based on your expertise and market demand.

Monetization Potential: Charging $150 per hour, working 20 hours per week, can result in $12,000 in monthly income.

Project-Based Contracts

For clients with specific needs or one-time projects, propose project-based contracts with a fixed fee. Clearly define the scope of work and deliverables to avoid scope creep.

Monetization Potential: Completing three projects per month at an average fee of $3,000 each can generate $9,000 in monthly revenue.

Performance-Based Fees

Incorporate performance-based fees tied to outcomes or results. This model aligns your success with the client's success and demonstrates your confidence in delivering value.

Monetization Potential: For improving a client's website conversion rate by 20%, charge a fee equivalent to a percentage of the increased revenue.

Subscription Models

Offer tiered subscription models with varying levels of access and support. Higher-tier subscribers receive additional benefits such as priority consultations or access to premium resources.

Monetization Potential: With 100 subscribers, charging $49 per month, you generate $4,900 in monthly recurring revenue.

The Future of Digital Consultancy

In conclusion, ChatGPT is ushering in a new era of digital consultancy services where expertise, personalization, and problem-solving converge to meet the evolving needs of businesses and individuals. As a digital consultant powered by ChatGPT, you have the unique opportunity to transform industries, empower decision-makers, and create a thriving income stream.

The future of digital consultancy is not just about offering advice; it's about being a trusted partner in innovation, problem-solving, and success. ChatGPT serves as your digital ally, providing instant expertise and personalization that can elevate your consultancy services to unprecedented heights.

So, as you embark on your journey in the realm of digital consultancy, remember that the possibilities are boundless, and the demand for your expertise is ever-growing. Whether you choose retainer fees, hourly rates, project-based contracts, performance-based fees, or subscription models, your impact as a

ChatGPT-powered digital consultant can be profound, and your income potential is limitless. The digital consultancy landscape awaits your expertise, and the future is in your hands.

Chapter 15: Navigating New Horizons and the Future of Opportunity

As we reach the culmination of this insightful journey, it's imperative to set our sights on the horizon and explore the dynamic opportunities that await in the ever-evolving realm of artificial intelligence (AI). The path we've traversed thus far has been illuminated by the boundless potential of AI, particularly ChatGPT. Yet, as we look to the future, we must recognize that the AI landscape is continually shifting and expanding, presenting us with new frontiers to explore and conquer.

The Unceasing Evolution of AI

The evolution of AI is nothing short of astonishing. What was once a nascent technology has now become an integral part of our lives, influencing nearly every facet of society. From healthcare to finance, from education to entertainment, AI is a transformative force that shows no signs of slowing down. ChatGPT, with its natural language understanding and generation capabilities, has been a harbinger of this transformative age.

In the chapters that preceded this one, we've witnessed how ChatGPT has been harnessed to create wealth, offer specialized expertise, provide personalized recommendations, and assist in problem-solving. Yet, the AI journey is far from over. We now stand at the threshold of a new era, poised to explore emerging trends, identify untapped niches, and continuously adapt to stay ahead.

Embracing Emerging Trends

To successfully navigate the future, it's imperative to embrace the emerging trends that are shaping the AI landscape. These trends not only define the direction in which AI is progressing but also present lucrative opportunities for those who can anticipate and capitalize on them.

AI in Healthcare

The healthcare sector is on the cusp of a digital revolution driven by AI. ChatGPT's ability to process vast amounts of medical literature and provide real-time information positions it as a valuable tool for healthcare professionals. Entrepreneurs and innovators can explore opportunities in telemedicine, health data analytics, AI-powered diagnostics, and medical research.

Sustainable Technologies

In an era of increasing environmental awareness, AI is being applied to sustainable technologies. This includes renewable energy optimization, waste reduction, climate modeling, and resource management. Entrepreneurs who invest in AI-driven solutions for sustainability not only contribute to a greener future but also tap into a growing market.

E-Commerce and Personalization

E-commerce is evolving with AI-driven personalization. ChatGPT can be used to create personalized shopping assistants that understand and anticipate consumer preferences. Entrepreneurs can capitalize on this trend by developing AI-powered e-commerce solutions that enhance the customer experience, increase conversion rates, and drive sales.

Education and EdTech

AI is revolutionizing education through personalized learning, intelligent tutoring systems, and automated grading. Entrepreneurs can explore opportunities in the EdTech sector by creating AI-driven educational content, tutoring platforms, or tools for educators. The demand for accessible and effective online learning resources is on the rise, making this a promising arena for innovation.

Identifying Untapped Niches

In the vast and ever-expanding AI landscape, there are countless untapped niches waiting to be discovered. Identifying these niches requires a blend of foresight, market research, and a deep understanding of emerging technologies.

Case Study: The Virtual Nutritionist Reimagined

Consider the story of Emma, a certified nutritionist with a passion for helping people lead healthier lives. Emma recognized that the traditional approach of providing dietary advice had limitations. To address this, she embarked on a journey to create a virtual nutritionist powered by ChatGPT.

Emma's virtual nutritionist offers personalized meal plans, tracks nutritional intake, and provides real-time dietary advice. Users can simply converse with the virtual nutritionist, share their dietary preferences, and receive customized recommendations. This innovative solution fills a niche in the market by offering accessible, affordable, and convenient nutrition guidance.

Emma monetizes her service through subscription plans, allowing users to access advanced features and ongoing support. The success of her venture highlights the potential of AI-driven solutions in niche markets where personalized, expert advice is in demand.

Monetization Potential: If Emma charges a monthly subscription fee of $20 and acquires 1,000 subscribers, she generates $20,000 in monthly recurring revenue.

Continuous Learning and Adaptation

To thrive in the ever-dynamic AI environment, it's imperative to adopt a mindset of continuous learning and adaptation. The AI landscape is marked by relentless progress, and those who remain at the forefront are the ones who embrace change with enthusiasm.

Case Study: The AI Educator's Odyssey

Meet James, an AI enthusiast who embarked on a journey to become a leader in AI education. He understood that staying updated with the latest developments in AI was paramount to his success. James decided to create an AI-driven educational platform where learners could access cutting-edge AI courses and stay abreast of industry trends.

James's platform leverages ChatGPT to deliver engaging and informative content. It provides regular updates on AI breakthroughs, real-world applications, and hands-on projects. By continuously adapting his platform to reflect the evolving AI landscape, James ensures that his learners receive the most relevant and up-to-date information.

James monetizes his platform through subscription-based models, offering different tiers of access to cater to learners with varying needs. The continuous learning aspect of his platform keeps subscribers engaged and eager to stay on top of AI trends.

Monetization Potential: With 5,000 subscribers paying an average of $30 per month, James generates $150,000 in monthly recurring revenue.

The Entrepreneurial Spirit in the AI Age

As we conclude this journey through the world of making money with AI, it's paramount to recognize that the entrepreneurial spirit remains alive and thriving in the AI age. The fusion of human creativity and AI capabilities has unlocked a realm of possibilities that were once deemed fantastical. Whether you're a seasoned entrepreneur or someone who is just beginning to explore the vast landscape of AI, remember these key takeaways:

- Embrace Change
  - The AI landscape is ever evolving. Embrace change, stay curious, and remain open to new opportunities.
- Identify Niches
  - Look for untapped niches where AI can make a meaningful impact.
  - Conduct thorough market research, identify pain points, and create innovative solutions.
- Monetize Creatively
  - There are diverse ways to monetize AI-driven ventures, from subscription models and project-based contracts to

performance-based fees and more.

- o Select the model that aligns best with your offering and target audience.
- Continuously Learn
  - o The world of AI is rich and multifaceted. Invest in continuous learning to stay ahead and provide value in your chosen niche.
- Innovate Fearlessly
  - o Don't be afraid to innovate and push boundaries. AI is a tool that amplifies human creativity; it's limited only by your imagination.

A Future Abounding with Possibilities

As we peer into the future, it becomes evident that the AI revolution is far from over — it's just beginning. Emerging technologies, novel applications, and uncharted territories await those with the vision and determination to explore them. The opportunities are boundless, and the entrepreneurial spirit is the compass that guides us through this exciting digital frontier.

In the chapters of your own life, how will you harness the power of AI to create, innovate, and prosper? The answer lies within you, ready to be unleashed in this limitless world of possibilities. As you embark on your unique journey, remember that the future is yours to shape, and the horizons of opportunity are vast and unexplored. With AI as your ally, the possibilities are, indeed, limitless.

www.ingramcontent.com/pod-product-compliance
Lightning Source LLC
Chambersburg PA
CBHW072217290526
45794CB00004B/1778